FOREWORD BY JONI LAMB

ARISE

The Journey *from* Fear *to* Faith

JANET BOYNES

ARISE!
By Janet Boynes

Published by Excel Publishers
600 Rinehart Road
Lake Mary, Florida 32746

Bible Gateway http://www.lockman.org/tlf/copyright.php (Message, New Living Translation, New King James Version, Amplified Bible)

Strong's Expanded Exhaustive Concordance of the Bible. Nashville: Thomas Nelson, 2009, s.v. "fall."

Merriam-Webster.com. Merriam-Webster, n.d. 1 Ap. 2014. http://www.merriam-webster.com/dictionary/change.

Cover design by Jason Johnson

Visit the author's website: www.janetboynesministries.com

International Standard Book Number:
978-1-62999-064-4

While the author has made every effort to provide accurate telephone numbers and Internet addresses at the time of publication, neither the publisher nor the author assumes any responsibility for errors or for changes that occur after publication.

First edition
13 14 15 16 17 — 987654321

Printed in the United States

FOREWORD

I love hearing testimonies about God's amazing power of redemption and transformation from our guests on *Joni Table Talk*. I often receive emails of how the guest's story moved the viewer to reach out to a God, who seems so far removed.

When Janet Boynes was a guest a few years ago, I was impacted by her story of how she overcame her struggles and her determination to help others. She came with a message of hope for those struggling with their identity and compassion without compromise.

In this book, *Arise,* Janet has created a workbook that takes you through a journey of questions for self-reflection and includes scriptures to guide and encourage. Her practical applications interwoven with her own story inspire you to be all that God created you to be.

This quote from chapter 3 stood out to me, "The best part of my story is that He did rescue me. He mended the broken pieces of my heart and He gave me a reason to live."

We who are in the body of Christ need to reach out to the hurting and provide not only teaching but practical resources that can be used in the process of transformation. I believe Janet has designed this book as a tool just for that purpose.

So pick up your pen, turn the page and begin your journey of transformation with Janet as she shares truth and revelation for those ready to embrace change.

Joni Lamb
Co-founder
Daystar Television Network

DEDICATION

We are so excited to share this *Called Out Devotional Workbook* based on Janet Boynes' book *Called Out*. This book has been in Janet's heart for quite some time and we believe it will open your eyes to God's truth about homosexuality.

We pray your journey will be deepened by the verses, prayers, and insight shared in these pages. Allow your heart to be open when you read this book, but more than that, allow the Holy Spirit to speak to your personal life.

CONTENTS

INTRODUCTION

*C*an you really leave homosexuality?

Yes, a thousand times yes, it is possible to leave homosexuality! I tell everyone I encounter about how *God's love* called me out. I believe my testimony, as told in my book *Called Out: A Former Lesbian's Discovery of Freedom,* has given hope to many who are considering or struggling with homosexuality. That is why I wrote the book, and that is why I wanted to offer a devotional/ workbook that would guide you in your journey.

I don't know your reason or motive for picking up this book, but I do pray that it gives you insight about who God is and about who He says you are!

Chapter 1
MASTERPIECE

Without a doubt, regardless of what you have been told, or maybe what you've never been told, you are a masterpiece created by God. You were created with purpose and there is greatness inside you. These are not just "motivational" words; these are truths that you can live by and see manifested in your life. Now, there is one who is incredibly threatened by the potential inside of you. Satan. His goal is to distort all that God stands for and cause you to believe his lies. If you are reading this book, you may have fallen for one or more of his lies. But if you press in with me, and allow me to shed light on the matter, you will experience something far greater than what the enemy of our souls has tried to offer you.

Psalm 139:13–16 teaches us (THE MESSAGE):

"Oh yes, you shaped me first inside, then out; you formed me in my mother's womb. I thank you, High

God—you're breathtaking! Body and soul, I am marvelously made! I worship in adoration—what a creation! You know me inside and out, you know every bone in my body; you know exactly how I was made, bit-by-bit, how I was sculpted from nothing into something. Like an open book, you watched me grow from conception to birth; all the stages of my life were spread out before you, the days of my life all prepared before I'd even lived one day."

KEY: This journey is not to define who we want to be, BUT to discover who we were created to be.

Most of us spend our time defining ourselves or allowing ourselves to be defined by others. Maybe your family had a role in defining who you are. This is a wonderful thing when what they say lines up with what God thinks of you, but what if what they spoke over you included things like:

- You will never amount to anything!
- I wish you had never been born!
- You are worthless!
- You can't do anything right!
- Is that the best you can do?

These words have been planted in the hearts of many and they could not be further from the truth. Man does not determine your value—your value comes from God, who thought you were worth His one and only Son going to the cross on your behalf.

Can you take a minute to think about words that have shaped and defined who you over the years? How did these words make you feel? Do you think they have had any power over you in how you see yourself, whether in a positive or negative light?

_____

_____

_____

_____

_____

_____

These words have a tendency to stay with us for a long time. They are like Post-it Notes that stick to us and with us through childhood and adolescence, and even after we enter adulthood.

Do you want to be set free from all the destructive words that have been spoken over you? I knew you would! Life and death are in the power of our tongue. Take a minute now to pray these words with me and allow the Holy Spirit to do His work in your heart. Write the word Lie over the destructive words that have been said against you in the lines above.

Prayer:

Father, thank You for creating me in Your likeness and for calling me Your own. I lay down every negative and hurtful word that has been spoken over me. They no longer have power over my life. I renounce them and whatever effect they ever had over me and I receive what You say about me and about my future. I rest knowing that I am fearfully and wonderfully made. In Jesus' name, amen!

Chapter 2
JUST AS YOU ARE

Our God is a God of miracles and love. I am living proof of that. And God is not a respecter of persons, what He has done for me He will do for you too, if you open your heart to Him. The closer I leaned into Him, the easier it became to see things His way. Communicating what I felt, what I needed, and what I thought, was crucial in my walk to freedom. I learned quickly that He wasn't shocked by my questions; rather, He was delighted that I had begun to include Him in my everyday decision-making. There was nothing I could hide from Him. At that point, I began to experience what the love of a father truly resembled and how He was eager to reveal Himself to me if only I'd ask.

Matthew 7:7–11 says (NLT):

"Keep on asking, and you will receive what you ask for. Keep on seeking, and you will find. Keep

on knocking, and the door will be opened to you. For everyone who asks, receives. Everyone who seeks, finds. And to everyone who knocks, the door will be opened. You parents—if your children ask for a loaf of bread, do you give them a stone instead? Or if they ask for a fish, do you give them a snake? Of course not! So if you sinful people know how to give good gifts to your children, how much more will your heavenly Father give good gifts to those who ask him?"

God loves it when we turn to Him in the midst of our pain and struggle. If you are a parent, you understand how profound this truth is. God wants us to run to Him and not run from Him. He isn't this old man with a long, white beard and a stick in His hand ready to beat you. He is a patient and gentle Father who will never tire of your requests for help!

KEY: We shouldn't be afraid to run to God, we should be afraid of being separated from God.

What is holding you back from reaching out to God? Are fear and/or shame preventing you from talking to God?

_____

_____

_____

_____

_____

_____

For me, walking away from God and living the homosexual life was fun, but only for a season.

TRUTH: Sin will take you further than you want to go, and keep you longer than you want to stay.

While I was away from God, I struggled with many negative emotions and my life was in complete turmoil. My list was probably much longer than the one below, but take a moment to analyze where you are in your journey and whether any of the things listed below have a hold of you?

HOPELESSNESS
HURT
DESPAIR
FRUSTRATION
LONLINESS
FEAR
DOUBT
DEPRESSION
DESPERATION
RESTLESSNESS
SHAME

I use to be afraid to fall asleep in case I died before I had turned back to God. I lived every day as someone I was not meant to be and my misery and attitude toward those around me and toward myself reflected that lie.

When you turn to homosexuality, you feel somehow twisted up inside causing all the emotions and feelings you checked on the prior page. It is like something isn't right. You think you are doing the best thing for yourself because that is what society says; that you were born that way and that you just need to accept yourself, but it just doesn't feel right. You lay awake at night and wonder if you will ever have a family. You try to imagine a different world in which homosexuality is perfectly normal. Then you try to imagine a different life in which you had chosen to get married and have children. You wonder if you have chosen the right way by choosing homosexuality— and then you realize you can't think of any way to leave it behind.

At times you hate God and wonder why He created you to begin with, and then later you wish there was some way He could rescue you from the living hell that torments you.

The best part of my story is that He did rescue me. He mended the broken pieces of my heart and

He gave me a reason to live. I know He can turn your list of hurting words to words of change, courage, peace of mind, hope, strength, acceptance, faith, and love.

Chapter 3
NOT ABANDONED

God's love can and will transform you, if you allow it to. It can bring you to a place of restored freedom. You don't have to make yourself perfect to call out God's name, to bury your head in His shoulder and cry the tears you've been holding back for so long. God doesn't work that way. He wants you to come to Him just as you are and He will help you fix your problems, rather than forcing you to fix them before He accepts you. Your willingness and obedience to go through the process can lead you to a change in your heart and mind.

When you are hurting so badly inside that you are willing to do anything, including going against what most of society considers normal by trying homosexuality, why not invest your time and effort in getting to know God's heart in the matter? It will lead you to know what love and acceptance really are, how to receive them in a healthy way, and discover the peace and freedom that can come from being satisfied in Him. I am not saying it will be easy, but I can say without a doubt that God will be with you through it all.

"This is what the Lord says—your Redeemer, the Holy One of Israel: 'I am the Lord your God, who teaches you what is good for you and leads you along the paths you should follow'" (Isa. 48:17, NLT).

Can you let that verse sink in for a minute? He will teach you and lead you!

"Your friend, the Holy Spirit whom the Father will send at my request, will make everything plain to you. He will remind you of all the things I have told you. I'm leaving you well and whole. That's my parting gift to you. Peace. I don't leave you the way you're used to being left—feeling abandoned, bereft. So don't be upset. Don't be distraught."

-John 14:25-27, The Message

That means you're not alone in this journey. You are not left to wander in the desert, you are not abandoned, and you are not asked to do this on your own strength! At times it might feel that way and in those times it is crucial to bring to remembrance the verses in His Word where He tells you that He will go before you (Deuteronomy 31:8), that He is your strength (Isaiah 40:31), and that if He is for you, no one can come against you (Romans 8:31).

Knowing in your heart that you are not facing your situation alone will give you the courage to overcome any and every obstacle you face. The God of the universe is looking after you. He says that you are the apple of His eye! Even as I write this, I can feel my chest fill up with enormous courage to run the race that is set before me! I know that *I can* because He is on my side! And I believe that you can as well!

Has there ever been a moment in your life when you felt abandoned by God? If you look back at that particular moment and compare it to this present time, do you now see things differently? Do you truly believe God has your best interest in mind?

_____

_____

_____

_____

_____

"'For I know the plans I have for you,' declares the Lord, 'plans for welfare {literally "peace"} and not for evil, to give you a future and a hope.'"

-Jer. 29:11, Amplified Bible

Chapter 4
THE SWITCH

"We are either in the process of resisting God's truth or in the process of being shaped and molded by His truth." — Charles Stanley[1]

Change of any kind can be scary, unpleasant, and terrifying. But it can also be just what you need to grow and experience life in a whole new level. I'm not here to convince you to "change" from gay to straight, or to give you a quick Five-Step Process to obtaining your freedom. It doesn't work that way. Change, (according to *Merriam- Webster's* dictionary), means "to make radically different." You can't change your actions and attitudes unless you change your thinking; transforming your mind is what the Bible calls it. It means to renew your way of seeing things and how you grasp them in your thoughts, to learn to discern the enemy of your soul's tricks and deceptions and to re-shape the way you see yourself to what He says you are.

At first, for the most part, what you feel and think may not align or match up to what the Bible says, and that's ok. Allow the Holy Spirit to work in your mind and heart while you do your own research in the Word. What does God have to say about homosexuality? What does He say about our bodies? Don't just take my word for it. Here is a list of Scripture verses you can read and search through to get a clear picture of what God says in regards to living a homosexual and/or immoral lifestyle:

- Leviticus 18:22
- Leviticus 20:13
- 1 Corinthians 6:9
- 1 Timothy 1:10
- 1 Corinthians 6:18
- 1 Thessalonians 4:3-5

What is the biggest change you've experienced in your live? How did you react to it? Have you grown from the experience?

_____

_____

_____

_____

_____

_____

"Real contentment must come from within. You and I cannot change or control the world around us, but we can change and control the world within us."

—Warren Wiersbe[2]

The temptations in your life are no different from what others experience. And God is faithful. He will not allow the temptation to be more than you can stand. When you are tempted, He will show you a way out so that you can endure. (See 1 Corinthians 10:13, NLT.)

In Matthew 11:28–30 (NLT) Jesus said: "Come to me, all of you who are weary and carry heavy burdens, and I will give you rest. Take my yoke upon you. Let me teach you, because I am humble and gentle at heart, and you will find rest for your souls. For my yoke is easy to bear, and the burden I give you is light."

You can lean on Him; He loves you so very much! I know it takes a lot of courage on your end, but the results will far outweigh the fear and captivity you now live with. In Jeremiah 29:11–14, when referring to captivity, God is talking about, in part, sin. Sin takes away your freedom because it calls you back to it again and again at the same time that is pulls you further away and separated from God. Sin becomes an addiction we cannot escape by ourselves. That's why God sent His Son, and that's why Jesus left the Holy Spirit here with us, and in us.

I know from life experience that when God calls, He calls in love. But sometimes the pain in life can be so bad that love seems only a far-off dream. Sometimes the hurt and shame in our hearts cuts so deeply that even hope seems impossible. I know that love can be found and hope can be renewed, but only if we turn to the One who truly loves us—God.

TRUTH: God never calls you by your shame—He always calls you by your name.

As you continue through this workbook, you will be stepping further into being transformed and making the switch in your mind. It is the kind of transformation that is positive and healthy and good; one that will bring healing and restoration to your heart. It is not an easy thing to put into practice, but so well worth it!

Chapter 5
NO SUGAR COATING

I will not mince words here, or make excuses—and the truth is you can't either. I want you to see homosexuality for what it really is, not the lie that tells you it is love, freedom, or the answer to all your problems. The Bible says that homosexual behavior is sin. It is not to be practiced. Leviticus 18:22 and 20:13 both call homosexuality detestable. Romans 1:26–27 calls it unnatural, and 1 Corinthians 6:9–10 says that homosexual offenders will not inherit the kingdom of God. The Bible leaves no wiggle room on the issue of homosexuality.

Christopher B. Davis[1] wrote on his blog May 10, 2013:

"To claim to be a 'gay Christian' (not a Christian struggling with homosexuality) would be equivalent to someone claiming to be a Christian Muslim or a Christian Satanist; it's oxymoronic. Two opposing

identities cannot coexist as one agreeable identity; that is schizophrenia. It is God's will that His born-again children be pure from sexual immorality, and anyone who rejects this rejects God."
(See 1 Thessalonians 4:1-8.)

If you are struggling with homosexuality and temptation, you are not alone. In different areas, aspects, and levels, we are all struggling with carnal desires and we have chosen to honor God with our lives in response to His love for us. We are all searching for something to fill the emptiness inside of us. Truth is, only God can because He put that emptiness there on purpose in the first place, with Him as the solution.

I pray that you are encouraged to seek the truth. I want you to be filled with hope rather than burdened with guilt. I want you to experience supernatural strength instead of trying to fight this in your own strength. I want to you to walk in the "joy unspeakable" the Bible talks about. All this is available to you! It is a gift. The more you seek Him, the more He will reveal himself to you. I pray that God's love will overwhelm you in such a way that you will never be the same.

---

[1] *Reprinted with permission.*

Chapter 6
STEPPING INTO CHANGE

$\mathcal{S}$tepping into change is taking a step-by-step move out of your comfort zone into unfamiliar and unknown territory. Don't be afraid, either, but be excited about the "discomfort of unfamiliarity" as you walk into victory. I am talking about uncomfortable situations that will cause positive change in your life. God wants you to come to a place where you experience a comfort that is secure, real, and peaceful.

Change requires faith. When you have faith in someone or something, you feel confident about their ability and goodness. Real faith will produce action. Do you trust and believe what God says about your life?

What does this look like in real life? Let me share some choices that I was faced to make when I made a choice to obey God.

1. **I walked away from everything.** Don't shoot me down just yet. I did what "I" needed to do in order to walk away from my partner and the life I was living. Was I fearful? Did I wonder what would happen? Was it a painful process emotionally and physically? Yes! The unknown can be scary, but remaining in the dark is far worse. Remember, He will never leave you, throughout it all He will meet you more than half way home. God is so faithful. Looking back now, I am convinced that that was the second best choice I've ever made. (First was inviting Jesus into my heart.)

   Pursing God will cause the chains that you feel trapped in to fall off. You are in control to make the change happen—your choices in partnership with His power will make all the difference.

2. **I reached out.** By nature, you and I crave connection with others. We were created to need each other. I knew early on that if I walked away from all that was familiar to me, I would need to have a group of people I could turn to. I had to get over myself, and ask for help. I stepped out of my comfort zone and reached out to others I knew could help and walk this new journey with me.

3. **I kept myself accountable:** I didn't like this word at first. Why should I give someone the right to call me out on something I was doing? This definitely goes against our human nature, I know, but there are so many benefits that came from doing this.

a. You receive encouragement: Who doesn't need someone cheering them on as they take on new adventures and set new goals? I know I did. And I know you will need someone (could be more than one) to lift you up when you are feeling depressed and lonely and you're thinking of giving up.

b. You get an honest opinion: The most important part of being accountable to someone is giving them permission to be honest and truthful with you. If an accountability partner is just patting you on the back or nodding their head when you make excuses, then they are not really holding you accountable after all. They should be comfortable telling you when you are getting off course or pointing out areas where you ought to focus more of your efforts.

c. It provides protection: Who do you think is more of an easy target? A person standing alone or a group of people standing together? Of course the person standing alone. When someone is standing in the gap for you and when someone believes with you, now that's a powerful thing. In Mathew 18:20 (Message Bible) it says when two get together on anything at all on earth and make a prayer of it, our Father in heaven goes into action. And when, "...two or three of you are together because of Me, you can be sure that I'll be there." That's His promise to you and me!

God will bring people into your life that will inspire and encourage you. But just remember, you are not expected to walk this out on your own.

Where are you in your current walk with God? Are you allowing people in your "space," or are you too afraid let others in? Is there anyone who you trust and go to for prayer and encouragement?

_____

_____

_____

_____

_____

Do you know that we are stronger together? In Proverbs 27:17 (NIV) it says, "As iron sharpens iron, so one man sharpens another." Ecclesiastes 4:9–10 (also NIV) tells us, "Two are better than one, because they have a good return for their work; If one falls down, his friend can help him up. But pity the man who falls and has no one to help him up!" God painted a beautiful picture for us to see that we need one another. This isn't a contest of who is better and holier; it is partnership among Christlike people who have captured the heart of God and who hold each other up while walking out this thing called life.

Can I encourage you to reach out to two brothers or sisters in Christ and share your heart with them? And then later, come back and write your experience here. (You can also e-mail me at info@janetboyesministries.com. I would love to know what your experience was like.)

_____

_____

_____

_____

_____

People do care

Just as you don't want to be judged and feel discarded, neither do they. You are in control of taking the steps, and God is with you just as He was with me. You may not know it at that time, but you will when you look back. Proverbs 16:3 (NLT version) says, "Commit your actions to the Lord, and your plans will succeed."

> *"A friend loves at all times, and a brother is born for adversity."*
> **—Proverbs 17:17, NIV**

Chapter 7
GOING SHOPPING

"Throw off your old sinful nature and your former way of life, which are corrupted by lust and deception. Instead, let the Spirit renew your thoughts and attitudes. Put on your new nature, created to be like God—truly righteous and holy."

-Ephesians 4:22–24, NLT

When grace found me, I was filthy, broken, and damaged. Let me explain. Having lived a lesbian lifestyle for fourteen years and having been raised in a dysfunctional home (seven kids, four different fathers) I can say that I was carrying lots of baggage. Probably enough to pack a plane... No, seriously!

My life was a mess, inside and out. Throwing off my old sinful nature was no joke. It was not easy. There were no "magic" words that made it all go away. (I wish!) I felt like an onion (stinky) and I could feel God peeling away (slowly and patiently) every layer of hurt, shame, hatred, un-forgiveness, and much more that I had piled up in my heart.

The process of transformation always begins within. At first, I was still dressing like a guy, but I knew God was working inside me. I could feel something was changing within my innermost being.

It has been a long journey to get to where I am today. I didn't turn from "gay" to "straight." I became whole. There are many heterosexuals who are walking around masking their wounds and struggles; they don't know that Jesus longs to make them whole as well. Can you accept the challenge to allow God to dig deep and peel away all that cripples you?

Let's go shopping in God's closet! Let's exchange our rags for his riches! These are some of the things He promises you:

JOY, UNSPEAKABLE-JOY
PEACE—THAT PASSES ALL UNDERSTANDING
EVERLASTING LOVE
GRACE—UNMERRITED FAVOR
MERCIES NEW EVERY MORNING

> *"For his anger lasts only a moment, but his favor lasts a lifetime! Weeping may last through the night, but joy comes with the morning."*
>
> **—Psalm 30:5, NLT**

What are some areas in your life that you would like to see change? And how to do plan to achieve those changes?

_____

_____

_____

_____

_____

_____

Prayer:

Father, Your Word tells us that we have the power with the Holy Spirit to cause positive change to happen in our lives. We ask You now to give us the courage it takes to step into change, the faith it takes to keep going, and the assurance of Your never-ending love for us so we never have to be afraid. Thank You that You would never cause any harm to come to us as we seek to put off the "old man" and be "renewed in the spirit of your mind." In the name of Jesus, amen.

Chapter 8
WHY ME?

$\mathcal{I}$f you are anything like me, you have probably battled with God countless times, asking, why me? Why did You allow this to happen to me? Why would You allow these feeling to grow in me? Why is it wrong to love someone of the same sex?

These questions, while completely understandable, come from a place of distrust and fear. As a child I'm sure your Mom told you various times not to put your hand on the hot stove. You might not have understood then what you know now, and the same thing applies here. He is not asking you to restrain yourself from sexual immorality because He wants to be a killjoy! He gives us these guidelines to live by so that we can enjoy a fruitful, prosperous, and healthy life. In our inability to see the full picture, we make wrong momentary choices that impact our future and that of those who follow behind us. When you take your eyes off of yourself and focus on Him, there is nothing you can't overcome with His strength! It's His ability doing beyond your ability. You will be able to achieve what you never thought you could.

I lived with homosexual desires for years, and I had asked God many times to take these feeling away. My life changed the day I asked God to help me overcome them. If God had taken away my same-sex attraction (SSA), He would have been doing all the work. By asking Him to help me overcome SSA, I acknowledged that I had some work to do as well. He was calling me—and is calling you—to be active participants in the work that He wants to do in our lives. Will you take the challenge of allowing God to show you what it means to overcome? As you read the Word, ask God for wisdom to understand what He wants to teach you about overcoming sexual temptation and about spiritual warfare.

"For whatever is born of God overcomes [author's emphasis] the world. And this is the victory that has overcome the world—our faith" (1 John 5:4, NKJV). *The Amplified Bible* says, "Little children, you are of God [you belong to Him] and have [already] defeated and overcome them [the agents of the antichrist], because He Who lives in you is greater (mightier) than he who is in the world!"

Let's break this down:

1. **You belong to Him:** you are His precious possession! I love how He makes it a point to tell us repeatedly that we belong to Him. He has no regrets. He is proud of the work of His hands.

2. **We have already overcome:** How is this possible? Jesus overcame! He sealed the deal. The same power that raised Him from the dead lives in you.

The fight has been fixed—your enemy already has been defeated! Now, lift up your head and walk like a victorious child of God, because you are.

What are some specific areas in your life that you need God's strength to overcome?

_____

_____

_____

_____

_____

Has your perspective changed when referring to overcoming rather than God removing the temptation?

_____

_____

_____

_____

_____

Chapter 9
THE TRUTH ABOUT SATAN

*E*arly in the book I stated that Satan is threatened by the potential inside you. This is true. To get a better understanding of this let me share how he is described in the Bible. Who is Satan?

"You were the model of perfection,
full of wisdom and exquisite in beauty.
You were in Eden, the garden of God.
Your clothing was adorned with every precious stone
red carnelian, pale-green peridot, white moonstone,
blue-green beryl, onyx, green jasper,
blue lapis lazuli, turquoise, and emerald
all beautifully crafted for you
and set in the finest gold.
They were given to you
on the day you were created.
I ordained and anointed you
as the mighty angelic guardian.

*You had access to the holy mountain of God
and walked among the stones of fire.*

*"You were blameless in all you did
from the day you were created
until the day evil was found in you.
Your rich commerce led you to violence,
and you sinned.
So I banished you in disgrace
from the mountain of God.
I expelled you, O mighty guardian,
from your place among the stones of fire.
Your heart was filled with pride
because of all your beauty.
Your wisdom was corrupted
by your love of splendor.
So I threw you to the ground
and exposed you to the curious gaze of kings."*
—Ezekiel 28:12–17, NLT

Lucifer is the name God gave him. He was perfection. He was full of beauty and wisdom; he had access to God and was blameless. I can't begin to imagine how magnificent Lucifer was, so much so that the Bible says he wanted to assume God's throne. (See Isaiah 14:13.) His pride led him to his fall. He, along with one-third of the angels that he deceived, was cast out of heaven. Second Peter 2:4 (NLT) says, "For God did not spare even the angels who sinned. He threw them into hell, in gloomy pits of darkness, where they are being held until the Day of Judgment."

Satan's goal is to kill, steal, and destroy all that comes from God and all that God represents. Here are some of the names the Bibles uses to identify Satan:

- Deceiver
- father of lies
- enemy
- accuser
- murderer
- tempter and ruler of the darkness.

He offers you fame and riches at the expense of your soul. He dangles the bait in your face so that you are enticed to sin while he plots to end your life. Remember, when you are being tempted, do not say, "God is tempting me." God never tempts anyone. Temptation only comes from one place and the Bible calls him—the devil—the tempter.

God placed Adam and Eve in the beautiful Garden of Eden. They were pure and morally innocent. They did not lack for anything physically, spiritually, or emotionally. They reigned over the garden with complete freedom and only one restriction: God commanded them not to eat from the Tree of the Knowledge of Good and Evil. One day, as Eve was standing near the forbidden tree, Satan appeared to her in the form of a serpent to entice her and drag her away from the things of God.

Think about when you are being tempted. Has Satan tempted you with a hamburger at a time when you are trying to lose weight? Or how about a cigarette in a time when you are trying to quit smoking? Perhaps he will tempt you with a woman or man you know you should not be involved with when you are trying to walk away from homosexuality? Or a liquor bottle when you are trying to go to rehab? Whenever you are trying to get help for something that is destructive in your life, the enemy will use anything he can to tempt you. He lives to lead God's people astray, to hold them captive, and to keep them in places of pain and despair. He has many methods of deception to discredit and contradict the Word of God. John 8:44 (NLT) says that Satan "was a murderer from the beginning. He has always hated the truth, because there is no truth in him. When he lies, it is consistent with his character; for he is a liar and the father of lies."

What was Eve's first mistake? She entered into a dialogue with Satan. His leading question opened the door that caused her to misinterpret God's Word to her. What is our mistake when we fall into sin? We engage into a dialogue with the wrong person or the wrong thing.

"Satan twisted God's words for his own purposes."
—Genesis 3:1, NLT

How many times do we know the truth, but twist things so we can engage in our lustful desires? The Bible says don't say you are tempted by God, you are tempted by your own lustful desires (James 1:13–15). The enemy is good about convincing us wrong is right and right is wrong.

Following in the footsteps of Jesus Christ should be more than just talk; there should be corresponding action. It ought to be a lifestyle that others around you can love about you and share in. We cannot use the devil to sin intentionally. Sin will take you further than you want to go and keep you longer than you want to stay. Yes, Satan is the ruler of this world and desires to lead us astray. But we have to choose to do the right thing. The Word of God can and will judge the intent and thoughts of your heart. (See Hebrews 4:11.)

God's Word will help us battle the forces of evil. After Jesus fasted forty days and forty nights, He was hungry and the devil came to Him and tempted him three different times. The devil isn't going to tempt us when we are strong; he will tempt us when we are tired, hungry, upset, or arguing with our spouses. Read Mathew 4:1–11. Jesus used God's Word to get rid of the devil. If Jesus had to do it, we do too!

Can you list a few of the lies the devil has gotten you to believe?

_____

_____

_____

_____

_____

_____

"Put very simply, Satan's power in the world is everywhere. Yet wherever men and women walk in the Spirit, sensitive to the anointing they have from God, that power of his just evaporates. There is a line drawn by God, a boundary where by virtue of his own very presence Satan's writ does not run. Let God but occupy all the space himself, and what room is left for the evil one?"

—Watchman Nee[1]

Chapter 10
LET IT GO

*G*rowing up with an abusive mom, and having gone through the neglect and mistreatment that I did, one of the questions I get asked all the time is "How can you forgive your mother after everything you went through?" It's easy for us to hold resentment and remain angry at those who have hurt and offended us. When we are inflicted with pain, the human response is to want to see that person hurt like we did, and pay for their wrong doing. While that is understandable, unforgiveness only hurts you.

To forgive is to stop feeling anger toward someone who has wronged you and stop requiring payment for what they did. When you forgive, you are not changing the past or diminishing what happened, but you are changing the future — your future.

You are probably thinking that you do not feel like forgiving. Forgiveness is not a feeling; it is a conscious choice. It is a decision you make that will benefit you and even those around you. Most of the time you might need to give your emotions time to catch up with the choice you made to forgive.

Thankfully, we don't have to do this on our own strength. We can continually depend on God to help us forgive. Ask Him to give you the grace to forgive even when it seems unfair and unjust.

Ephesians 4:32 (NLT) says: "Instead, be kind to each other, tenderhearted, forgiving one another, just as God through Christ has forgiven you."

Luke 12:48 says: "to whom much is given, much is required." This statement is often used to refer to a person who in is a position of power or wealth and God often requires more of them. But we can also apply this to forgiveness. We have been forgiven much. I know I have! In the same way, much is required of me; the grace and mercy that has been offered to me I should be offering others.

Honestly, the best way to get back at those who have hurt you is to forgive them. Let's look at Proverbs 25:21-22; "If your enemies are hungry, give them food to eat. If they are thirsty, give them water to drink. You will heap burning coals of shame on their heads, and the Lord will reward you."

You're probably saying there is no way that you're going the extra mile for those who have hurt you! Let me tell you what can cause you to have a change of heart —praying for your enemies! When you begin to sincerely pray for those who have hurt you, you will feel a sense of freedom and relief and you will begin to see them with different eyes. They have probably experienced a lot of pain and hurt in their lives. Remember, hurt people hurt people. God can even use you to bring healing to their heart as well.

Matthew 5:43-47 (MSG) says; "You're familiar with the old written law, 'Love your friend,' and its unwritten companion, 'Hate your enemy.' I'm challenging that. I'm telling you to love your enemies. Let them bring out the best in you, not the worst. When someone gives you a hard time, respond with the energies of prayer, for then you are working out of your true selves, your God-created selves. This is what God does. He gives his best—the sun to warm and the rain to nourish—to everyone, regardless: the good and bad, the nice and nasty. If all you do is love the lovable, do you expect a bonus? Anybody can do that. If you simply say hello to those who greet you, do you expect a medal? Any run-of-the-mill sinner does that."

We often forget that being forgiven has a lot to do with forgiving others. In Matthew 6:12 (NLT) it says: "and forgive us our sins, as we have forgiven those who sin against us." This is a two way street, they go hand in hand. We are forgiven in the same way that we forgive others. It is unmerited and undeserved but we are called to do it.

If we want to truly experience a life of freedom, a life that is prospering in every aspect, we need to come to grips that God's way is the best way. Forgiving the offender brings you inner peace and joy. Jesus forgave those who had wrongly accused Him, beaten Him, and hung Him on the cross. One of His last words were "Father forgive them". This was a deep and profound expression of His Love for us!

You might be struggling to forgive someone who molested you and took advantage of you, or maybe someone who abandoned you in your time of need. No matter what the situation was or is, forgive them. Find the courage to let go and take hold of the reward God offers you. He is your defender. He has your back.

Who have I not been able to forgive?

_____

_____

_____

_____

_____

_____

Prayer:

Jesus I ask you to help me forgive _____. Give me the strength and the Grace to choose daily to forgive them. Holy Spirit guide and teach my heart to let go of all anger, resentment and hatred. Work in my life and allow me to see them as you do. I know I can do all things through you! In Jesus name, amen.

Chapter 11
FROM FAILURE TO GLORY

Let's look at Micah 7:7 (NLT): "As for me, I look to the Lord for help. I wait confidently for God to save me, and my God will certainly hear me. Do not gloat over me, my enemies! *For though I fall, I will rise again*. Though I sit in darkness, the Lord will be my light" (author's emphasis). When I fall, I will arise. God does not give us any choice about this one. Strong's Concordance defines the word fall here as "falling short or failing," and this could be in any arena of human effort. It can be in your business. It could be in a relationship. It could be a moral failure.

Actually, the word I think most specifically applies to a moral failure is morality. Morality is defined in *Merriam-Webster's Dictionary* as "firm adherence to a standard of behavior." And unfortunately for much of the world, there is no standard. We live in a predominantly amoral society whose people have given themselves over to moral relativisms, situational ethics, and the like. For a believer, for you and for me, the standard of behavior that we are to steadfastly follow is the principle of God's Word. So when we talk about a fall, really in any arena, sadly many people never arise.

Many people find it hard when the pain of failure has been nonstop over a period of time and you're not easily willing to put yourself through that kind of pain again. As a result, they never arise. Failure begins to define who they are and limits their destiny accordingly. Failure cannot define who you are or what life holds in store for you unless you allow it to. *The mandate is to arise.* Don't ever settle for something less than you know is the best. When you fall and you feel like you don't want to risk going through that pain and heartache again, know that that's the enemy of your soul working on you with deceptions and traps. That's when you have to grit your teeth, get up off the floor, and arise.

Of course, it requires much more than my simply saying, "You've got to get up." Let's take a moment and consider wrong behavior as opposed to right behavior. The Word of God is our moral standard. It tells us how we should live out our lives. You're ultimately responsible for your behavior. Yes, the grace of God works with us; but it does not assume the responsibility of life for us. The grace of God works with us and enables us to do what we've decided to do.

Behavior is a primary result of the dominant desires that reside within a person's heart. Desire is the main motivating force behind any pattern of behavior. People who consistently behave in a particular way reflect the desires that burn most intensely within them. Often, we find wrong desires and carnal desires, prompting behavior that is in conflict with the Word. This was true in my case. What I desired and what I believed didn't line up. Life gets a lot smoother if we can coordinate our desires with the Word of God. If we can diminish wrong desires, turn up the heat on right desires—which would be in line with the Word of God—then we're motivated to behave with consistency in line with the principle of God's Word.

So how do you alter desire? The things you desire most are the things you think the most about; it's that which dwells within your mind that you see yourself doing. Even without being consciously aware of it, you cannot desire something you've never thought about. But once you begin the process of mental consideration, thinking about it becomes a more frequent pattern of thought making the desire become greater. So that's why the Lord says you're going to have to cast down wrong or vain imaginations. (2 Corinthians 10:5 NLT.) You have got to do it. I will add that there are some God-given desires that the enemy perverts. I mean, you can take something straight out of the Bible and the enemy is going to try to push it to one ditch or the other if he can. So it's not just things that are obviously wrong with the Word. Prosperity is an example. It is the will of God that you prosper. It is not coincidental that every person wants to see their family's needs met and have something a little beyond that. That's a godly desire. The enemy is going to labor to push it to a ditch. For instance, craving to be rich is the beginning of a great deal of pain and heartache in someone's life. Our approach to money needs to be as a resource to God's purpose. And then we'll enjoy things richly along the way, according to His Word. So desires that have been twisted need to be de-intensified in your thought life and cast down. You need to get your thinking right.

Some people have problems with pornography because in some instances that's all they think about and it becomes such an obsession that they cannot get away from it. And in some cases, it's more addictive than some drugs. So taking these thoughts captive is an absolute necessity if you're going to be able to alter wrong behavior.

There is no point in arising if you don't correct what made you fall. Evaluating the main contributor to the failure and getting your thought life right about that particular thing is crucial. It will be hard to do if you've never tried to control a particular line of thought or pattern of thought. Initially you will find yourself having to concentrate on it minute by minute. But like anything else, God created us to establish patterns and habits. Once you begin taking your thoughts captive in a particular area, it may seem hard but trust me, as you are faithful to do that and take those steps, it will become more natural to you and there will be certain patterns of thought eventually that you reject out of hand. You won't even go there anymore, because that's the way God has made us to function. So it's not something that you should shy away from because of the initial difficulty. If we're going to arise, we have to identify contributors to the failure and make the alterations necessary to come back to our moral standard.

Now we can talk about arising. How far do you want to arise? Do you just want to get it back to the status quo that you used to be? Do you want to get just a little bit better than that? God wants you to set goals that are consistent with His will. We see in Isaiah 60:1 "arise…" We start off with the same word, arise. Arise and let your light shine. Light is a reference to God's purpose for your life and the glory of the Lord is risen upon you. His glory, His majesty, His power, His exaltation will be demonstrated through your life. Really, failure should be viewed not as a hindrance to the will of God, in my opinion, but a springboard to the glory of God. But you have to see yourself in light of the Word. If you see yourself just as someone who just wants to get out of trouble, you see yourself as more of a failure than you do a success, at least in terms of past experience. You've got to see yourself through the promise God has enabled you to walk in. You are sealed by the blood of the Lamb and you can do all things through Christ who strengthens you. (Study Phil. 4:13.) This should then help us set marks that are meaningful. Arise. Shine. It doesn't matter who you are or what you've done. When failure occurs, you can't stay there. God doesn't give you that option. He says you shall arise. Get up. And begin setting your sight and your mark toward what He says you can be in Christ.

Keep your thought life captive. Make the changes that are needed. Make the adjustments to your behavior that need to be made and focus on it today. Let tomorrow take care of itself. You do the best you can do today. Forget that which is past. Take no thought about tomorrow. Do the best you can do today. When tomorrow comes, do the best you can do tomorrow, which is now today. And just keep living a day at a time.

Now, of course, it's by the grace of God that we can raise to a level of His glory. There are natural alterations you need to make and spiritual changes you need to initiate. Naturally you may need to adjust your attitude or your money management practices. You will want to go higher than that in God; as high as you can and it takes His grace to do that. You can't work your way there on your own.

There are spiritual things that have to be a part of this process and appropriating His grace is the major consideration. Paul was having some real problems. He was failing to have the impact he desired and persecution was coming at him in a way we can't even imagine. And God said, "Paul, my grace is sufficient unto you" to lift him beyond the difficulties he was dealing with and to take him higher in the plan and purpose of God.

The Bible tells us that grace, God's unmerited favor, is received first of all by faith. You have to believe that it's available to you and believe that you can operate in it. And then know that grace has the chance of having an impact on your life. Faith is the first consideration. You have to believe you can rise above a moral failing. You have to believe you can fulfill all the will of God. And then the grace of God is your enabling ability to do so.

I think there is one other major factor we do not talk enough about where grace is concerned. Let's look at 1 Peter 5:5: "In the same way, you younger men must accept the authority of the elders. And all of you serve each other in humility, for 'God opposes the proud but favors the humble.'" This is about God's grace to do what you couldn't otherwise do; grace to overcome every evil tendency. Grace to enable you to arise above the pain of the situation you may face right now. Grace is not available to anybody but the humble. Verse 6 says, "So humble yourselves under the mighty power of God, and at the right time he will lift you up in honor." And of course, humility is something that we would all claim to have, when in fact there's a touch of pride in certain areas of most of our lives. You can always identify where it is and do something about it. He gives grace to the humble. It also says give all your worries and cares to God, for He cares about you. When you carry cares, you no longer trust the Lord. You no longer believe that God is going to change these things and you have made it impossible for grace to operate because you have to believe in order to appropriate grace. Fear, cares, and anxiety are your indicators you do not believe the right thing. Cares simply suppress what God has already put within you.

If you are born again, God put within you the capacity to experience great joy. Cares keep the joy from bubbling up. In Philippians 4:8 we have another reference to our thought life when it says, "...therefore brethren, think on these things." Think only on these things; things that are lovely and pure and of a good report. It's only when we have these kinds of thoughts that any virtue and power can be released. Grace brings the power that enables you to bear change in your life.

The Bible says you have the mind of Christ, so you don't have to figure out how to become more joyful or how to get the peace of God to work in your life. All you have to do is to get rid of the cares. It is a discipline that needs to be practiced and developed. You are not secure in the privacy of your mind anyway; God knows everything you're thinking about. What you think most about produces the strongest desire, which as we discussed earlier is the primary governor of behavior. So once more, we have the need to cast down wrong and vain imaginations and take every thought captive to the obedience of Christ. This includes not only things that are contrary to God-given desires, things that perhaps would be the product of carnal desire; but also things that produce fear or anxiety or create the taking of cares.

You can do the hardest things imaginable in this life without focusing your imagination; your capacity to mentally focus your mind upon the consequence of things not working out like you want. You can do it. And if you're going to arise out of the failures we all experience on a daily basis, it's a must that we comprehend the importance of what we do with our minds.

Your mind is like a filter for what goes into your heart.
—**Unknown**

You do realize the enemy of your soul can't access your heart, correct? Only you and God can access your heart. Satan has no ability to invade your spirit, to impact your spirit, or your heart. He has to come through your mind, and you're the one who controls your mind. The things that you think the most about drop down into your heart, and if you have been thinking the wrong things, that will produce negative fruit. Do you see the importance your thought life has when it comes to rising?

1. How do you feel every time you fall?

_____

_____

_____

_____

_____

_____

2. Do you believe His grace is sufficient (strong enough) for you?

_____

_____

_____

_____

_____

_____

3. How can you apply the lesson here to your
   personal life and situation?

   _____

   _____

   _____

   _____

   _____

   _____

Chapter 12

MIRROR MIRROR ON THE WALL

*I*n this final chapter, I want to encourage you to be real and transparent with yourself and God (and recall, He already knows). You can only fix and mend the areas in your life in which you recognize and acknowledge that there is need. Self-honesty is the ability to take a clear and fresh look at yourself and your situation. Within seeing oneself objectively, one is able to determine where one stands in relation to one's honesty, even and especially if, one observes something one does not like and would rather not see. You may not like what you see, as was the case for me, but let that be your stimulus and motivation to pursue God.

Look at this verse with me: "Don't fool yourself into thinking that you are a listener when you are anything but, letting the Word go in one ear and out the other. *Act* on what you hear! Those who hear and don't act are like those who glance in the mirror, walk away, and two minutes later have no idea who they are, or what they look like. But whoever catches a glimpse of the revealed counsel of God—the free life!—even out of the corner of his eye, and sticks with it, is no distracted scatterbrain but a man or woman of action. That person will find delight and affirmation in the action" (James 1:23–25, MSG). In the physical, my life was slowly being transformed. This is what I used to look like:

I didn't get rid of my manly clothes in one night. I constantly renewed my mind to the mind of Christ. Looking in the mirror now, I am a completely different person. As I surrendered my will to God, I finally gave Him the opportunity to work in my heart and He had a chance to work on my innermost desires so that at the end of my process and journey they would match His desires for me. Most importantly, the person I saw in the mirror, the one that no one else could see, was no longer broken and hurting. I no longer saw loneliness and fear in my eyes. I was no longer looking at a picture of myself—I now saw Jesus.

When you look at the mirror, what do you see?

_____

_____

_____

_____

_____

_____

1. Have you been open and honest about your weakness? If not, why not?

_____

_____

_____

_____

_____

_____

2. What are your struggles and temptations?

_____

_____

_____

_____

_____

_____

3. What are the things that cause you to stumble and in what ways can you ask for help?

_____

_____

_____

_____

_____

_____